*Inspector's standard weights dating from about 1800.*

# WEIGHTS AND MEASURES
# AND THEIR MARKS

## A guide to collecting

### J. T. Graham FITSA
*revised and with additional information on marks by*
### Maurice Stevenson FITSA

### Shire Publications Ltd

# CONTENTS

*Published in 2003 by Shire Publications Ltd, Cromwell House, Church Street, Princes Risborough, Buckinghamshire HP27 9AA, UK. Copyright © 1979 by J. T. Graham; 1987 and 1993, executors of J. T. Graham and Maurice Stevenson. First published 1979. Second edition 1987; third edition 1993; reprinted 2003. Shire Album 44. ISBN 0 7478 0226 2.*

Printed in Great Britain by CIT Printing Services Ltd, Press Buildings, Merlins Bridge, Haverfordwest, Pembrokeshire SA61 1XF.

British Library Cataloguing in Publication Data: Graham, J. T. Weights and Measures and Their Marks: Guide to Collecting. – 3Rev.ed. – (Shire Albums; No. 44) I. Title II. Stevenson, Maurice III. Series 389.15. ISBN 0 7478 0226 2.

ACKNOWLEDGEMENTS
Thanks are expressed to Mr D. W. Ellis, Curator of the Avery Historical Museum at Smethwick, for providing and permitting the use of many illustrations; also to Mr R. Holdaway, Mr C. A. Peal, Mr J. R. Roberts and Mr H. Robinson for access to specimens, photographs and records of their own collections. Permission to use photographs previously published in *Antique Collecting* and *Antique Finder* by the Antique Collectors' Club of 5 Church Street, Woodbridge, Suffolk, is gratefully acknowledged as also is the work of Mr F. Done of Knutsford in photographing specimens. The late Mr M. Stevenson expressed his gratitude for assistance in the collection of information on marks to the British Academy, the Department of Trade and Industry, Dr D. Vaughan of the Science Museum, Rosemary Weinstein of the Museum of London, Mr M. A. Crawforth, Mr G. Gordon, Mr R. G. Willey, Mr C. Ricketts, numerous museum curators and all others who have assisted in the quest. The cover photograph was taken by Dr David J. Stevenson.

COVER: *(Top, from left) Publican's gill, half-gill and quarter-gill pewter measures, Victorian; apothecaries' 2-drachm, 1-drachm and ¹/₂-drachm aluminium weights, Edwardian; milkman's half-pint 'dipping' measure, 1911; flat-round brass weights 2 oz, 1 oz and ¹/₂ oz, stamped crown over MW (Manor of Wakefield), about 1890; brass bell weights 1 lb, 8 oz and 4 oz, as used by grocers and butchers, Victorian. (Lower, from left) Public house pint drinking pot of Mocha ware, about 1902; iron ring-weight with lead round ring staple for adjustment and stamping, eighteenth/nineteenth century type; (upper) flat-round 4 lb iron weight by the Coalbrookdale Company, made soon after the introduction of Imperial weights and measures, 1826; (lower) flat-round 1 lb copper/bronze weight, stamped crown over W and Founders' Company marks, William IV 1832-6; iron ¹/₂ lb 'bar' weight, about 1920; public house pint drinking pot decorated with 'Scenes from coaching days', about 1914.*

*A selection of small apothecaries weights. Note that two are marked 'drams' instead of 'drachms', an earlier alternative spelling later applied exclusively to avoirdupois drams.*

# WEIGHTS: HOW OUR SYSTEMS STARTED

When a standard of weight was developed for the first time it had to be based on something which could be easily obtained and which was of a uniformly found weight. In the millennia before Christ the bases for weight standards in the Mediterranean and Indian centres of trade were variously the seeds of the liquorice plant and of the carob, a leguminous plant. These seeds were very hard when fully ripened.

Weights were made from these seeds, mostly of stone, but for weighing more precious goods like gems or gold dust other materials such as haematite and nephrite were then used. The stone weights were often flattened balls or domes. In Greece and some other countries early weights were also made of lead but because lead is soft these are not so often found.

In Britain the use of weights and the development of standards was much influenced by trade with Europe although earlier the Romans had introduced their own systems during the occupation. The word *pound* is derived from the Roman

*libra pondo* and *ounce* from the Roman *uncia*.

The basis for standardisation was a grain of wheat and this seed, commonly used in Europe during the middle ages, became the *grain* weight on which the present systems are built. Because of the complications in Britain's domestic and foreign trade there were at times no less than six different pounds, each containing different numbers of grains. The *tower pound*, used for testing coins, weighed 5,400 grains; the *troy pound* for gold and silver was 5,760 grains; a *wool pound* was 6,992 grains and three others for weighing ordinary goods varied between 6,750 and 7,680 grains.

The confusion which existed was partly straightened out when Elizabeth I decided that the only pound for weighing ordinary goods should be one of 7,000 grains and that the troy pound should be used for precious metals and stones.

When King John signed the Magna Carta he had agreed that there should be only one weight and one measure but we see that there were still two pounds, for

3

different purposes. In 1758, however, Parliament decided to legalise just one, the troy pound. The word *troy* is believed to have originated from a weight used in the town of Troyes in France. The larger pound was called the *avoirdupois pound,* sometimes spelled *averdepois,* i.e. for weighing heavy goods. Eighteenth-century scientists made three weights of 5,760 grains but before one of them could be legalised as the one Imperial Standard Pound George II died and that standard was not installed until 1824. Theoretically all traders should then have started using the troy pound for all purposes but they preferred the 7,000 grain pound and carried on using it.

The new Standard Pound was kept with the Standard Yard at the House of Commons. In 1834 a stoker burning a quantity of wooden tallies (money counting sticks) in the cellars of the House accidentally burned the whole building to the ground. The Standard Troy Pound was never seen again. Scientists then set about creating a new pound and because the troy pound was unpopular it was decided to create the Imperial Standard Pound of 7,000 grains — as Elizabeth I had ordered two centuries earlier. The troy pound continued in use for its original purpose, however.

Until recently there was a third system in use in Britain, the apothecaries' system, again based on the grain weight. Weights in this series are specially interesting because of the peculiar symbols, originating from early medical practice, to denote the parts of the apothecaries' ounce.

BELOW: *A set of brass bell weights. If they are examined for matching points it will be seen that the smaller weights are of different designs.*

4

*A set of flat-circular brass avoirdupois weights. The figures '94' on the 1 lb weight stand for 1894.*

# SIZES AND SHAPES OF WEIGHTS

To meet the very different needs of different trades there has had to be a wide variety of different-sized weights available. Elizabeth I divided the avoirdupois pound into 16 ounces, each of 437.5 grains. This ounce was divided into 16 *drams*, eight making half an ounce.

The troy pound, however, was always divided into 12 ounces – the Roman *uncia* means one-twelfth. Trade reference to a troy *pound* was made illegal in 1878 and trade could therefore only continue in the troy ounce of 480 grains, one-twelfth of 5,760 grains.

The apothecaries' system was also based on the troy weight system, each ounce also weighing 480 grains. These ounces were divided into 8 *drachms*, not drams, of 60 grains each. Each drachm was divided again into 3 *scruples* of 20 grains. There were intermediate weights of 2 scruples (40 grains) and 1½ scruples (30 grains).

The troy and apothecaries' systems (the latter having now gone metric) were used only by jewellers, bullion merchants and chemists. All other trade dealings were in the avoirdupois system and it was in this that almost up to the end of the nineteenth century there was the greatest confusion about the sizes and shapes of weights used. Today the system provides for the following weights series: 56 lb, 28 lb, 14 lb, 7 lb, 4 lb, 2 lb, 1 lb – lb being an abbreviation of *libra*. Below this series come: 8 ounces (oz), 4 oz, 2 oz, 1 oz, ½ oz (8 drams or dr), ¼ oz (4 dr), 2 dr, 1 dr and ¼ dr.

The reason for these spaced-out denominations is to avoid the confusion which arises between weights of very close denominations. Before legislation prevented it in 1878 traders used what suited them and what was available and might (with naughty intent) use 13 lb weights alongside 14 lb weights or 3 lb with 2 lb. These oddly denominated weights can still be found and make interesting additions to a collection.

Anyone starting to collect weights might be advised to collect single weights of different sizes, shapes or materials

ABOVE: *Note the maker's name and verification stamps on these flat-circular brass weights.*

LEFT: *The weights shown above are here seen nested.*

rather than hope to buy complete sets or incomplete ones with the idea of completing them. Complete sets of brass bell weights are becoming expensive and even then, many have been made up from odd weights. This can be ascertained by examining closely the shape of the handle, the shoulders and the number of incised rings at the base.

Avoirdupois weights can be found in a variety of shapes and perhaps the *bell* weights are the most attractive. Other shapes are the *flat-circular* weights, which are never in bigger sizes than 7 lb. Like bell weights they are made in brass and in circular iron but they can be 'nested'. Flat-circular iron weights below 4 oz are usually only household weights sold with cheap kitchen scales. *Bar* weights come in all

sizes from 56 lb to 1 oz. The *ring* weight, once seen in post offices bearing the broad arrow, is a truncated pyramid, like the bar weight always in iron but with a ring at the top for lifting. Older weights of this sort are sometimes found with lead run round the ring for adjustment but iron and brass weights made since 1890 have a round or rectangular hole underneath for adjustment and to receive the verification stamp. Household weights are generally distinguishable by their rough appearance and lack of an adjusting hole.

Old troy weights were usually of nesting or 'cup' shape but modern examples are normally cylindrical in the larger sizes and flat sheet brass or aluminium in the very small sizes, ending in aluminium wire for the smallest. Apothecaries'

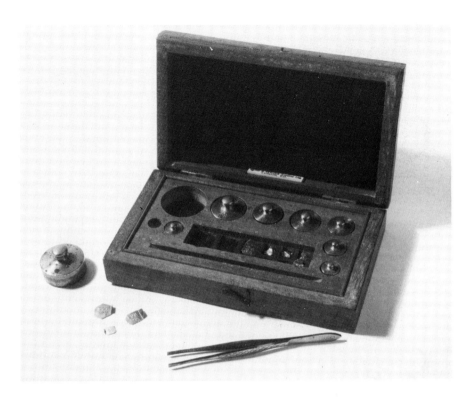

ABOVE: *A box of small metric weights as used by a pharmacist.*

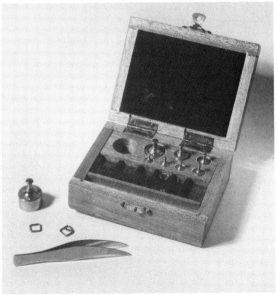

RIGHT: *Apothecaries' weights. Note the long necks or knobs to avoid confusion with metric weights.*

7

ABOVE: *Two iron 'bun' weights of about 1890.*

BELOW: *Two iron 'bar' weights of around 1800 to 1830.*

weights in the larger sizes are very like troy weights and not unlike smaller metric weights.

The *cental* series, which came into use about 1880, runs down from 100 lb through 50, 20 and 10 to 5 lb, which is the smallest in the series. These weights are octagonal bar weights to avoid confusion with ordinary bar weights. Metric iron bar weights are hexagonal.

Some early weights have no indication of their weight on them but most do. This may be in full, as *One Pound*, or as *1 lb, 8 oz, 14 lb* etc. During the nineteenth century some weight manufacturers made their name on the weight larger than the denomination. The name of a maker called Pound on an 8 oz weight or Stone on a 7 lb weight could be confusing if the name letters were larger than the actual denomination. This practice was stopped in 1907.

Weights of 7 lb upwards made of stone were used, from the seventeenth to the nineteenth centuries, for assessing the tax on salt, by farmers and in the wool and coal trades. These weights were usually of limestone, or granite dressed to a cylindrical, square or pear shape. See the chapter on pitfalls.

Some very interesting weights to collect are pottery weights, many manufactured by Wedgwood, but they were made illegal in 1907 because they were liable to chip and lose weight. They also had

TOP: *Pottery weights as well marked and perfect as these are very desirable.*
ABOVE: *Four attractive brass cylindrical weights of about 1900.*
rather large adjusting holes filled with lead, and these probably brought about dishonest practices. The printing is put on by underglaze transfer and is usually a greeny blue. They can be found in the series from 14 lb down to 1 oz.

9

ABOVE: *Brass weights with Founders and City of London marks. Left to right: George III, William IV, George IV.*

LEFT: *An Elizabethan 4 oz weight. Note the crown over 'EL', the ewer and 'A'.*

BELOW: *Two 'cased' weights filled with lead, of about 1875.*

*An iron 'pie-shaped' weight, a registered design of 1847. Note the rejection 'star' on the copper plug.*

# INTERESTING MARKS ON WEIGHTS

As early as Anglo-Saxon times there were laws requiring weights and measures to be tested and stamped with an official mark to prevent dishonest dealing. A crown over the ruling monarch's initial was the most usual mark of approval but local verification marks derived from civic arms or the authority's name were also frequently used.

During the middle ages, and before the concentration of heavy industry in the Midlands, most weight manufacturers were located in the London area. City of London officials tested and stamped bronze and brass weights at the Guildhall jointly with the Worshipful Company of Founders from 1579. Similarly, under a Charter of 1611, the Plumbers' Company was empowered to test and stamp lead weights and iron weights requiring the addition of lead for final adjustment. Although extensively used in earlier days, very few lead weights bearing the Plumbers' Company stamp of St Michael

holding scales in the left hand and sword in the right along with the Guildhall dagger and royal cipher have survived. They were banned finally in 1835.

Many of the more durable bronze weights continued in use without much deterioration from the reign of Elizabeth I, and later, and are still to be found. Up to 1826, when a new law took effect, brass and bronze weights made or used within 3 miles (4.8 km) of the City of London boundaries were stamped with four marks: the City dagger and crown over royal cipher; the Founders' 'laver-pott' or ewer and A for avoirdupois.

From 1826 until the Founders ceased to exercise their ancient right late in the nineteenth century, the figures 18 and 26 appeared with the Founders' ewer and collectors should not be misled by this date. At the same time the City of London changed from the dagger to the full City arms, with the shield and dagger in the top left quarter.

11

Before the introduction of uniform numbered stamps in 1879 a great variety of local stamps was used by provincial authorities. Illustrations of many of those based on local arms can be found under 'Verification marks' on pages 24-8. Many more used crown over royal cipher and the town or county initials. These are more difficult to identify unless a later numbered stamp is present to provide a clue. In some instances the same initials were used by different authorities: for example, CH signified the counties of both Hereford and Huntingdon as well as the Corporation of Hastings. The city of Bristol used CB over a C but also at times over a G, while Cambridge County used the letter C by itself below district letters AD, CD, LD and ND. In Surrey, where large numbers of weights and measures were stamped in the mid Victorian period, various arrangements of the letters SY were used in combination with district initials such as AE and WA. Other unusual combinations include Wk over Hl or Kl for districts of Warwickshire, BSM for Borough of St Marylebone and MW for Manor of Wakefield, which was used in Wakefield and Halifax up to the time of the surrender of the manor's ancient rights in 1893.

A list of stamp numbers issued by the Standards Department of the Board of Trade between 1879 and the end of Edward VII's reign (1910) can be found on pages 30 and 31. Figures and letters were often added separately to indicate the date of stamping: for example, E/13 would indicate the fifth month (May) of 1913 and A/29 the first month (January) of 1929. The overmarking of a verification stamp with a six-pointed star means that the weight has been deemed to be unfit for further use in trade.

The word *solid* on a brass weight means that it is made entirely of brass rather than being a shell of brass filled with lead which could easily be tampered with. Lead-filled weights are sometimes marked *cased,* but in case of doubt they can be detected by tapping with a small hammer; they give out a dull note rather than a metallic ring. From 1842 to 1883 many manufactured goods, including weights, carried a diamond-shaped *registration mark.* This indicated that the design had been registered with the Patent Office and gave copyright protection for a period of three years. An example of an iron 'pie-shaped' weight bearing a registration mark is shown on page 11. The mark can also be found on brass lozenge-shaped apothecaries' weights of mid nineteenth-century origin. Apothecaries' weights were denominated by symbols and Roman numerals as follows:

| | |
|---|---|
| 4 drachms ............................ | ʒ iv. |
| 2 drachms ............................ | ʒ ij. |
| 1 drachm ............................ | ʒ i. |
| 2 scruples ............................ | ℈ ij. |
| 1½ scruples, or half a drachm ...... | ʒ β |
| 1 scruple ............................ | ℈ i. |
| half a scruple ......................... | ℈ β |

Postal weights date from the introduction of the penny post in 1840 and many of the earlier ones were cased rather than solid. From about 1852, when there were half-ounce units for letters called *postages,* some postal weights were marked with P over a figure to denote the number of postages. Thus P over 4 meant 2 oz and P over 2, 1 oz. Postal weights marked ⅓ and ⅔ oz date from 1869 in pursuance of an Anglo-French agreement.

*Top left is a modern form of the bell weight, about 1967. The weight on the right dates from about 1870. The two postal weights below could be as early as 1860.*

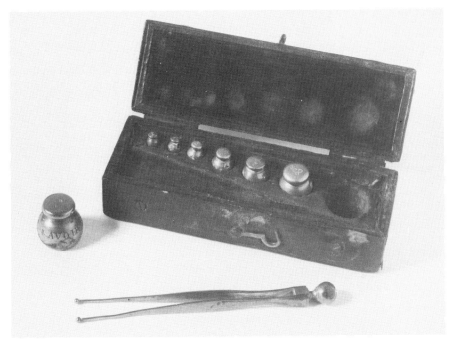

*An inspector's box of small testing weights, about 1910.*

# WEIGHTS FOR TESTING WEIGHTS

## INSPECTORS' WEIGHTS

Basically all trade weighing and measuring equipment has to be made to an approved pattern or design and once the equipment is in use it needs to be tested again from time to time.

To do this inspectors have their own sets of weights and measures and those they take out every day are called *working standards*. Other sets of standards which stay in their office, called *local standards*, are solely for checking that the working standards are still correct. The local standards themselves are tested at regular intervals by officers from the appropriate government department against *their* standards, which in turn are tested periodically against other standards held in their possession. At the end of this chain of interdependence are what used to be called the Imperial Standards (one mentioned as being lost in the

House of Commons fire) but these are now described as definitions in terms of the immutable International Metric Standards.

The small weights in a box illustrated above are, by their size and shape and the presence of a pair of tweezers, either local or working standard weights. A sure sign is the mark of a portcullis or chequerboard, the original stamps of approval of the department once responsible for testing inspectors' weights (see Verification marks). Spherical weights are almost always working or local standards. Small adjusting holes underneath are usually capped with brass plugs and if the name of the authority which used the weights appears they are the more desirable.

Many local authorities are now placing their surplus standard weights and measures in museums as metrication and the reduced number of local authorities puts them out of use.

13

ABOVE: *Testing a weighbridge about 1925. Note the 56 lb bar weights. The steam roller is put on to help check the machine at its highest capacity.*

BELOW: *A more modern method than that shown above. The weighbridge is tested by using 5 cwt block weights in a cradle.*

14

LEFT: *A 7lb bronze wool weight of Charles I, about 1630.*

RIGHT: *A 14 lb bronze wool weight of George I, about 1715.*

## WOOL WEIGHTS

Wool was taxed in medieval times: in 1467 the tax was one penny on the *tod* of 28 lb. The tax assessor, called a *tronager*, travelled his district carrying two 7 lb or 14 lb weights slung over his saddle-bow. These were used for testing the wool merchants' scales, which were called *trones*.

The earliest known wool weights were flattish shields of lead or bronze with a hole at the top for a carrying thong. They bore, incised, the royal cipher and arms. When new weights were supplied the old ones were destroyed. After 1587 the royal arms were moulded. In 1590 the Founders' Company of London was allowed to stamp wool weights with a 'laverpott' or ewer, resembling a coffee pot, which may appear two or three times around the bottom of the weight. Genuine wool weights have a shallow circular depression at the back, drilled out, no doubt, for final adjustment.

From about 1600 there are at least four marks which can be found on these weights, some appearing more than once. These are: the ewer; a Roman A for avoirdupois; a dagger and a royal cipher. Other marks could include the maker's or tronager's own mark, his name or district mark and some emblem or symbol of his town or city. Some of these marks can be seen in the photographs above.

The form of the royal arms on these weights changed generally with succeeding monarchs from Elizabeth I through to George III, at the end of whose reign they went out of use. Cromwell's weights had St. George and the Irish harp and no royal arms. They were stamped with the shield of St George in place of the crown over royal cipher. The booklet *Weight Stamping by the Worshipful Company of Founders and the City of London* contains illustrations of all these marks.

15

TOP LEFT: *Half Moidor, seventeenth century.*
TOP RIGHT: *Half Guinea, William III.*
BOTTOM LEFT: *Crown, or Quarter Unite, James I.*
BOTTOM RIGHT: *Quarter Guinea, George III.*

## COIN AND BANK WEIGHTS

As gold and silver coins had intrinsic value weights were needed to check that they had not lost value from wear or interference.

During the eighteenth century many Portugal Pieces were in circulation along with the guinea and demand by merchants for pocket scales and weights greatly increased, especially after 1776 when the official weight of the guinea was increased slightly.

Collecting coin weights is a specialist subject but some idea of the variety of weights covered can be gained from those illustrated.

*Brass bank weights for weighing bags of sovereigns, dating from about 1885.*

*Elizabethan nested troy standards of 1588.*

# MEASURES: MATERIALS AND SHAPES

Much of what has been said about the development of weights and the way in which they are marked after testing applies also to measures. The interest in measures, therefore, is in their variety.

Before the seventeenth century most measures in ordinary use were of wood for it was not until that period that pewter was cheap enough to come into common use. Measures made of leather of earlier date do not often survive. The earliest wooden measures were turned from the solid and very liable to split. Their use for liquids was forbidden in the early eighteenth century and thereafter they have continued to be used only for the sale of dry goods such as corn, peas and garden seed.

The commoner wooden measures are made from thin wood steamed into a cylinder, the overlapping ends nailed or dovetailed together, with a circular base fitted into the bottom of the cylinder. To prevent the bottom being fraudulently removed and replaced the measure was stamped with a hot branding iron which fitted both base and inside. Some of these measures are found without any marks and may have been hand-made by the intending user. Genuine measures will all have a denomination (e.g. peck, gallon etc) and a royal cipher or town mark of one date or another. They are all subject to woodworm attack.

PEWTER MEASURES

Pewter is a soft metal made mainly from tin, with lead and sometimes a little copper or other hardening material. Silver occurs in pewter only by accident and therefore there is no such metal as silver pewter as some believe. Sixteenth-century pewter was heavy because it contained a large proportion of lead but in succeeding centuries a much lighter pewter evolved. From 1907 pewter was not allowed to contain more than ten per cent lead.

Pewterers were required to register their *touch*, that is their trademark, and

ABOVE LEFT: *The 'Stirling Jug', the standard of the Scottish pint (about three Imperial pints) made in bronze c. 1500 and entrusted to the Royal Borough of Stirling.*

ABOVE: *Probably from a large nested set of cup weights, this weight is marked '14 oz 11 pennyweights 16 grains', equalling an avoirdupois pound of 7,000 grains. About 1750.*

LEFT: *Verification stamps branded inside a wooden measure.*

BELOW: *Six Victorian dry measures. Those with handles are turned from the solid.*

18

*Irish 'haystack' pewter measures dating from about 1830.*

this mark generally took the form of a design incorporating their name or a symbol by which their work could be identified. H. H. Cotterell's *Old Pewter, Its Makers and Marks* contains over six thousand of these marks.

A measure or vessel with a lid or cover is described as a *tankard;* those without a cover are *mugs.* Old pewter takes on a bloom or patina with age but when it was new it could be polished to look almost like silver. It adds to the interest of a measure if it bears what are called *false hallmarks.* These marks were put on by the maker, quite illegally, in order to give the impression that the measure was made of silver; the centre photograph on page 20 shows marks not unlike a crowned leopard's head and a lion rampant.

As to whether old pewter should be brought back to its original condition by polishing, the author feels that what has been acquired by years of handling and atmospheric action should not be removed. Cleaning pewter should be limited to washing in lukewarm soapy water, drying and buffing with a soft cloth—as with silver.

Some guidance as to the age of a measure can be had by noting the shape of the handle, the style of the thumbpiece to the cover, the height of the cover, the outline of the body and the number and position of the rings or fillets encircling the body. Specialist books explain this in more detail but dating is always only approximate. A dated inspector's stamp will also help.

Pewter is easily dented and the measures doubtless came in for a lot of rough treatment in alehouses, where they where used for both measuring and drinking. Dents could be knocked out, however, and for this a *pewter jack* was used. The alehouse keeper would probably send a number needing repair strung together by their handles. To ensure that his measures were not mixed with others, his name or the name of his inn, or both, would be inscribed on the base of the measure. These inscriptions make a very interesting collecting feature though difficult to display. Some measures have glass

19

bottoms. The usual story about this is that they enabled drinkers to keep an eye on their drinking companions whilst satisfying their thirst but this was probably no more than a ploy to discourage drinkers from banging measures on the table.

Small pegs protruding inside a measure allowed the publican to sell part of the quantity marked on the outside or friends to share a pint. Some very small measures marked *20, 22* etc were used for serving out spirits, the figure indicating the fraction of a pint measured to the brim.

Another interesting feature of pewter measures, occasionally also met with in glass and pottery measures, is the insertion of a false or double bottom. These measures will never be found stamped by an inspector as their purpose was to defraud, even if only to enable the barmaid to drink less when invited to 'have one'. Some glass 'measures',

TOP: *Two pewter measures with jacks made for removing dents.*

ABOVE: *False 'hallmarks' on a pewter measure.*

BELOW: *Pottery measures by John Tams of Longton, Staffordshire.*

known as *deceptives*, are so moulded that they appear full when containing less than they purport to hold.

## POTTERY MEASURES

A number of jug measures made from about 1880 onwards by the firm of John Tams of Longton in Staffordshire are illustrated on page 20. The most interesting of these are those which carry a lead verification plug in the base. Another interesting feature is that a hollow protrusion at the top of the handle was provided to be ground off to bring the vessel to a better accuracy. Similar jugs and mugs, also those of Mocha ware with 'fern' or 'tree' decoration, were made by Maling of Newcastle upon Tyne and other unidentified potters. These had the inspector's verification mark stencilled by sandblasting the outer glaze. This stamp can often only be seen by tilting the measure to catch the light and as a result many are sold as ordinary mugs because the stencilled mark is barely visible. This field of collecting has not yet attained high popularity and consequently prices are still reasonable.

## OTHER MATERIALS

Copper conical measures can be obtained in sizes from half a pint to 5 gallons. They were mostly used by wine merchants. Generally ignored, but an interesting field, are the 'tin' conical measures now so seldom seen on garage forecourts for measuring oil, each with some advertising matter displayed. Other measures made from sheet metal or tin are milk dippers from the early twentieth century. All these carry a verification stamp impressed either on the measure or on a pad of solder.

An interesting collection can also be made of glass measures, all of which were again stencilled with the inspector's stamp but which are unlikely to date earlier than 1880. These include beer measures and cylindrical and conical glass measures used by pharmacists and scientists. Some of these latter graduated measures can be found without an inspector's stamp but collectors should exercise their knowledge of early glass before accepting that unstamped measures date from before 1880.

*A set of Burmese Hentsha (chicken) weights; each weighs half the weight of the next larger. About 1920.*

*A selection of eighteenth-century cup weights. The largest weight is frequently lidded.*

# PITFALLS FOR THE COLLECTOR

## WEIGHTS

Modern recasts of English and foreign brass bell weights are easily recognisable by the roughness of the casting and by lack of finish or patina. No genuine weight will have rough or sharp edges as they would all have been rubbed off with wear. Look inside crevices and holes for roughness. Bad pitting and small blow-holes are other signs of fakes.

Flat-circular iron weights with a slot cut into the centre are not technically weights but counterpoises to be used with or on platform machines without dials. These usually weigh from an ounce to a pound but are marked *equals 14 lb* or *56 lb* or *1 cwt*, as the case may be. Even so they can be collected.

Weights are made today as souvenirs for the tourist trade in the Far East and travellers should look for signs of lack of wear on any metal weight. Burma, however, adopted the metric system about 1949 and so some weights can have been genuine trade weights and not just souvenirs. Tourists in the Middle East will certainly be offered weights but antiquities are normally not exportable from those countries and small balls of stone are easily copied. This applies also to West African Ashanti weights purporting to be of gold or bronze and in the shapes of axes, hammers, combs, pipes, elephants and the like. If genuine these are highly desirable but there are many copies.

Nests of weights were mostly made at Nuremburg from the sixteenth century onwards. They can be either troy or avoirdupois or German, Dutch or French. Normally, each cup is half the weight of that in which it rests and the lidded cup weighs as much as the remainder put together. The smallest is always solid and most frequently missing or has been replaced by some made-up piece. The difference in colour of the metal is often a sign of replacement. These weights are today very skilfully reproduced and aged and one needs to have examined a number of genuine specimens before making an expensive purchase.

Wool weights are also known to be copied but as they are usually reproduced from an original the moulding is flat and not crisp and copies almost never have the shallow depression at the back.

It is not good policy to buy boxes of weights or nests of cup weights where some are missing as it is hardly ever possible to find suitable replacements.

Stones with a ring in the top may have been made by a farmer to hang on his harrow. Genuine stone weights should be well shaped, should have some sign of a denomination cut into the side or top and the ring ought to be embedded in lead, which might have a mark on it. But stone weights in salt areas suffered greatly by corrosion.

## MEASURES

Much of the faking is applied to copper and pewter measures. Copper measures, like copper kettles, are imported to Britain by the thousand from Europe and the Middle East every year. Some are treated with acid, dented and given other signs of age. Some are recognisable as fakes because the seam under the handle is too perfect — older measures usually have a cramped or zigzag-soldered or brazed seam. The handles do not have enough substance and the inside of the measure generally lacks staining, verdig-

ris and genuine well embedded dirt. An impressed mark immediately under the handle is a fairly certain sign that the article has been imported. Regrettably some of these fakes also carry forged inspectors' stamps.

Old pewter is becoming so expensive that it is well worth the faker's time to treat new pewter. New pieces are being reproduced with old touch-marks — these often show only part of the touch and most frequently *London* or *Dublin*. The pewter is distressed by ill treatment of every kind.

Confusion in dating can also occur from the crown over WR verification stamps, which originally stood for William III and started to be used in 1700 under a law of that date, but which continued to be put on measures until the law was repealed in 1824, even though subsequent monarchs had different initials.

An old piece needs to be examined carefully for cracking seams, pewter rot, holes, soldered-on handles, repairs and other damage which lessens desirability, but faked pewter is often in such good condition even after treatment that it needs special attention. Sometimes the only safe indication of newness is that the edges of rims are still too sharp.

Some beautiful stoneware jugs and mugs were produced in the eighteenth century at Fulham, Mortlake and elsewhere and many of these had a WR mark of verification. The guide to any question of reproduction is to handle as many genuine specimens as possible and to see authenticated examples in museums and then to think twice before buying.

# VERIFICATION MARKS

## LOCAL STANDARDS

Since the reign of Henry V, and probably earlier, local standards were issued through the Exchequer and were marked with royal insignia. From about 1660 up to 1866 they were stamped when verified with a chequerboard in addition to the crown and cipher of the ruling monarch. On bronze measures of capac-ity each mark was struck twice on the top rim in diametrically opposing positions. From 1866 when the Standards Department of the Board of Trade took over the verification of local standards, the chequerboard was replaced by a portcullis surmounted by a date. This should not be confused with the earlier portcullis stamp of Westminster.

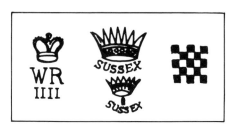  

*(Left) Exchequer marks on local standard weight of 1834 alongside old Sussex stamps. (Centre and right) Board of Trade verification stamps for standard weights, measures and scales.*

## CITY OF LONDON AND GUILD COMPANY 'HALLMARKS'

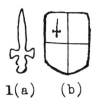    

1(a)   (b)      2(a)      (b)      3      4

*(From left) 1(a) London Guildhall 'dagger' as stamped, with royal cipher and 'A' for avoirdupois, on bronze and brass weights up to 1826; (b) full city arms used from 1826 onwards. 2(a) Founders' Company 'ewer' as stamped with Guildhall marks on bronze and brass weights up to 1826; (b) as marked from 1826 into the late nineteenth century. 3. Plumbers' Company 'St Michael' as stamped with Guildhall 'dagger' and royal cipher on lead weights and some iron ring weights from 1611 onwards. 4. Reputed Goldsmiths' Company 'lion' found on some troy pennyweights of late eighteenth-century origin.*

## TOWN AND COUNTY STAMPS

The illustrations on the following pages have been drawn from impressions of actual stamps, photographs, rubbings or other well authenticated sources. Sizes are usually much smaller than shown, about ¼ inch (7 mm) overall being about the average. The forms illustrated were not invariably followed, replacement of stamping punches accounting for some of the differences, according to the idiosyncrasies of the maker or inspector. Some of the variations are referred to in the notes which follow the illustrations.

ABERDEEN

BASINGSTOKE

BRADFORD

CHATHAM

ARBROATH

BATLEY

BRIGHTON

CHESTER

ABINGDON

BEDFORD Cº

BRISTOL

COLCHESTER

AIRDRIE

BERKSHIRE

BUCKINGHAM Cº

CONGLETON

ARGYLL Cº

BERWICK Cº

BURY ST EDMUNDS

CORNWALL

ARUNDEL

BIRMINGHAM

CAITHNESS Cº

COVENTRY

AYR

BOSTON

CARLISLE

CUMBERLAND

25

DENBIGH Co.

EXETER

HADDINGTON

ISLE OF ELY

DONCASTER

FIFE

HAMPSHIRE

ISLE OF MAN

DORSET

GATESHEAD

HANLEY

KENT

DOVER

GLASGOW

HIGHAM FERRERS

KIRKCALDY

DUDLEY

GRANTHAM

HUDDERSFIELD

LANARK

DUNFERMLINE

GRAVESEND

HULL

LANCASTER

EDINBURGH

GRIMSBY

INVERNESS

LAUNCESTON

LEEDS

MACCLESFIELD

NORFOLK

QUEENBOROUGH
(KENT)

LEICESTER

MAIDSTONE

NORTHUMBERLAND

READING

LINCOLN

MANCHESTER

NORWICH

RUTLAND

LINCOLNSHIRE

MIDDLESBROUGH

NOTTINGHAM

SAFFRON WALDEN

LIVERPOOL

MIDDLESEX

PETERBOROUGH

1848
ST ANDREWS

LONDON (CITY)

NEWBURY

PLYMOUTH

PORTSMOUTH

SALISBURY

TOWER OF
LONDON LIBERTY

NEWCASTLE-
UPON-TYNE

SHEFFIELD

27

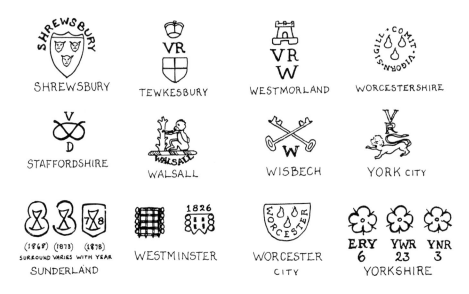

SHREWSBURY  TEWKESBURY  WESTMORLAND  WORCESTERSHIRE

STAFFORDSHIRE  WALSALL  WISBECH  YORK CITY

(1869) (1873) (1878)
SURROUND VARIES WITH YEAR
SUNDERLAND

WESTMINSTER

WORCESTER
CITY

ERY  YWR  YNR
6    23   3
YORKSHIRE

Alternative stamps to those illustrated were used by the following authorities: *Bury St Edmunds:* the letter B over S, with another (variable) letter above. *Chatham:* the Kent horse with the letters C.P. (Chatham Port) below. *Cornwall:* crown over CC with district letter below. *Cumberland:* crown over VR above C and a district number. *Gateshead:* the castle by itself. *Glasgow:* the letter G with DG (Dean of Guild) and district number. The name abbreviated over a date, for example, *GLAS:* over 58 (1858). *Huddersfield:* the ram's head stamp illustrated was adopted on the incorporation of the borough in 1868 and used until the uniform stamp (number 51) was issued in 1879. *Isle of Ely:* the W over crossed keys denotes Wisbech Division. Crown over I of E was also used. *London City:* some pewter measures of seventeenth to nineteenth century origin were stamped with the letters HR or WR flanking the city sword or shield. All later stamps incorporated the city arms in a shield or circle along with the crown and royal cipher. From 1879 onwards the allotted number 2 was included with the city arms and royal insignia. *Manchester:* from 1844 the stamp consisted of the words 'City of Manr' inscribed in a circle below VR and crown with a date, for example, B 57 (February 1857) in the centre. *Middlesex:* the district numbers and inspector's initials, for example M for Morrison and F for Faulkner, sometimes appear above the shield. As the arms of Essex also consist of three scimitars, Middlesex stamps have been mistakenly attributed to Essex, whose stamps however were either crown over ESSEX, or EX above a district number. *Newbury:* another inspector's name, T. LONG, was also incorporated in the stamp.

## NUMBERED STAMPS

The lists on the following pages show the allocation of verification stamp numbers as it was in 1910, the last year of Edward VII's reign. Most of these numbers are still in use by the authority named or its successor but since 1946 the numbers have been increased from 636 to about 1650 to allow one for each inspector.

By referring to the lists, collectors and others interested can find the town or county using a particular number between 1879 and 1910. The lists also provide a fairly good, but not entirely reliable, guide to stamps originating between 1910 and 1946.

The period in which markings were effected can be seen from the royal cipher. Thus, all crowned VR stamps date from between 1879 and 1901 while crowned ER stamps date from 1901 to 1910. Typical examples of these stamps are as follows:

*From left: design officially recommended in 1879; form generally adopted; as adopted by the City of London; as adopted by the London County Council on its formation, 1892; usual form 1901 to 1910; as marked by sandblasting on pint and half-pint beer glasses.*

In the absence of a date mark (see 'Interesting marks on weights') there is nothing to distinguish the GR stamps of George V from those of George VI. These cover the years 1911 to 1952 (no change was authorised during the brief reign of Edward VIII). The official design for Elizabeth II had the digits 'II' inserted between the E and R but in 1969 a new regulation decreed that in future all verification stamps should consist of a crown over number only. Examples from the period 1911 to 1969 are:

*Varying surrounds as sometimes used. Examples from City of Birmingham (from left) 1934, 1935 and 1936, form prescribed in 1952, modern form prescribed in 1969.*

29

OFFICIAL STAMP NUMBERS

Where a name is shown in italics in the following lists the number alongside had become obsolete (that is, taken out of use) by the year 1907. These numbers and those described as 'unappropriated' have since been re-issued, mainly in the years immediately after 1946.

Numbers marked with an asterisk had previously been in use by another authority, as follows: 9, Bedford County 1879 to 1890; 58 to 63, Chester County 1879 to 1894; 84, Stratford-upon-Avon 1879 to 1894; 113, Oxford County 1879 to 1907; 203/204, Ayr County 1879 to 1907; 269, 271, 273 to 276, West Suffolk 1880 to 1891; 280, Kent County 1881 to 1906; 358, Kent County 1879 to 1890; 368 to 375, Oxford County 1879 to 1890; 389, 390, Surrey County 1879 to 1890; 411 to 415, Gloucester County 1882 to 1894; 421, Pembroke County 1882 to 1891.

| Number | District |
|---|---|
| 1 | Formerly used by Board of Trade |
| 2 | London, City |
| 3 | Edinburgh |
| 4 | London, County |
| 5 | Manchester |
| 6 | Birmingham |
| 7 | Nottingham |
| 8 | Bedford, County |
| * 9E | Cornwall Eastern Division |
| 9W | Ditto Western Division |
| 10-13 | *Bedford, County* |
| 14 | Bradford |
| 15 | Banff, County |
| 16 | Renfrew |
| 17 | Renfrew, County |
| 18-19 | Derby, County |
| 20 | Margate |
| 21 | London, County |
| 22 | Forfar, County |
| 23 | Coatbridge |
| 24-25 | Lanark, County |
| 26 | *Ditto (obsolete)* |
| 27 | Maidstone |
| 28 | London, County |
| 29 | Middlesex |
| 30 | London, County |
| 31 | Middlesex |
| 32-33 | Stafford, County |
| 34-36 | Glasgow |
| 37 | Sheffield |
| 38 | Bath |
| 39 | Bedford |
| 40 | Beverley |
| 41 | Hull |
| 42 | Canterbury |
| 43-44 | Cumberland |
| 45-48 | *Ditto (obsolete)* |
| 49-50 | Westmorland |
| 51 | Huddersfield |
| 52-53 | Lanark, County |
| 54-57 | Chester, County |
| * 58-62 | Glasgow |
| * 63 | Unappropriated |
| 64 | Sunderland |
| 65 | Wolverhampton |
| 66-67 | London, County |
| 68 | Devonport |
| 69 | Perth, County |
| 70 | Wigan |
| 71 | Newcastle-on-Tyne |
| 72 | Paisley |
| 73 | Perth |
| 74 | Poole |
| 75 | *Saffron Walden* |
| 76 | Salford |
| 77 | *Sandwich* |
| 78 | *Ramsgate* |
| 79 | Salisbury |
| 80 | Scarborough |
| 81 | *South Molton* |
| 82 | Stafford |
| 83 | Stalybridge |
| * 84 | Unappropriated |
| 85 | Kings Lynn |
| 86 | Birkenhead |
| 87 | *Exeter, City* |
| 88-102 | Lancaster, County |
| 103 | *Ditto (obsolete)* |
| 104-109 | Lancaster, County |
| 110 | Leicester |
| 111 | Montrose |
| 112 | Norwich |
| * 113 | Unappropriated |
| 114-116 | *Buckingham, County* |
| 117 | Buckingham, County |
| 118-119 | *Buckingham, County* |
| 120 | Oxford |
| 121 | Chester |
| 122 | Dumfries, County |
| 123 | Brechin |
| 124 | Weymouth |
| 125 | Ely, Isle of |
| 126-127 | *Ditto (obsolete)* |
| 128 | *Wisbech, Borough* |
| 129 | *Lincoln, County* |
| 130 | Lincoln, County |
| 131-143 | *Lincoln, County* |
| 144 | Grantham |
| 145 | Derby |
| 146 | Aberdeen |
| 147 | Liverpool |
| 148 | Darlington |
| 149 | Plymouth |
| 150-152 | Yorks, North Riding |
| 153 | Unappropriated |
| 154-155 | Durham, County |
| 156 | Northampton |
| 157 | Durham, County |
| 158-160 | *Dorset, County* |
| 161 | Dorset, County |
| 162 | *Ditto (obsolete)* |
| 163 | Dorset, County |
| 164-166 | *Ditto (obsolete)* |
| 167-173 | Sussex, West |
| 174 | Leeds |
| 175-188 | *Essex, County* |
| 189 | Essex, County |
| 190 | Sutherland, County |
| 191 | Roxburgh, County |
| 192 | *Sudbury* |
| 193 | *Calstock* |
| 194 | *Bodmin* |
| 195 | *Bury St Edmunds* |
| 196 | *Buckingham* |
| 197 | Brighton |
| 198 | Boston |
| 199 | Bolton |
| 200 | Blackburn |
| 201-202 | Ayr, County |
| * 203-204 | Unappropriated |
| 205 | *Andover* |
| 206 | *Aldeburgh* |
| 207 | Colchester |
| 208 | Coventry |
| 209 | Fife, County and Burghs of Anstruther and Dunfermline |
| 210 | *Devizes* |
| 211 | *Worcester, County* |
| 212 | *Dunstable* |
| 213 | Greenock |
| 214 | Hereford, County |
| 215-216 | Sussex, East |
| 217 | Hove |
| 218 | Eastbourne |
| 219 | Unappropriated |
| 220 | Chepping Wycombe |
| 221 | Worcester, County |
| 222 | *Huntingdon* |
| 223 | Ipswich |
| 224 | Kidderminster |
| 225 | *Kidwelly* |
| 226 | Kilmarnock |
| 227 | Kinross, County |
| 228 | *Tenby* |
| 229 | Kirkcudbright, County |
| 230 | Orkney, County |
| 231 | Kirkwall |
| 232 | Louth |
| 233 | *Lyme Regis* |
| 234 | *Liskeard* |
| 235 | Newark |
| 236 | Newport (Mon) |
| 237 | *Oxford* |
| 238 | *Sanquhar* |
| 239 | London, County |
| 240 | Elgin, County |
| 241 | *Tenterden* |
| 242 | *Thetford* |
| 243 | *Totnes* |
| 244 | Tynemouth (North Shields) |
| 245 | Walsall |
| 246 | Great Yarmouth |
| 247 | *Yeovil* |
| 248 | Linlithgow, County |
| 249 | Newbury |
| 250 | Hastings |
| 251 | Galashiels |
| 252 | Cardiff |
| 253 | *Sutton Coldfield* |
| 254 | Reading |
| 255 | Penzance |
| 256 | Rothesay |
| 257 | Bute, County |
| 258 | Inverness, County |
| 259 | Brecon, County |
| 260 | Unappropriated |
| 261 | *Bideford* |
| 262 | Berwick-upon-Tweed |
| 263 | *Callington* |
| 264 | Worcester |
| 265 | Southampton |
| 266 | Huntingdon, County |
| 267-268 | Suffolk, East |
| * 269 | *Govan* |
| 270 | West Bromwich |
| * 271 | Lossiemouth |
| 272 | Suffolk, West |
| * 273 | Ossett |
| * 274-276 | Unappropriated |
| 277 | Warrington |
| 278 | Bootle |
| 279 | Barrow-in-Furness |
| * 280 | Unappropriated |
| 281 | Southport |

| | |
|---|---|
| 281 | Stranraer |
| 282 | *Pevensey* |
| 283 | Anglesey, County |
| 284 | *Deal* |
| 285-287 | Glamorgan, County |
| 288 | *Ditto (obsolete)* |
| 289 | Glamorgan, County |
| 290 | Clitheroe |
| 291 | Windsor |
| 292 | Nairn, County and Burgh |
| 293 | *Anstruther Easter* |
| 294 | Irvine |
| 295 | Oban |
| 296 | Swansea |
| 297 | Lincoln |
| 298-302 | Yorks, West Riding |
| 302-302a | |
| & 302b | Dumbartonshire |
| 303-304 | *Yorks, West Riding* |
| 305-307 | Yorks, West Riding |
| 308-309 | *Ditto (obsolete)* |
| 310 | Yorks, (West Riding |
| 311-320 | *Ditto (obsolete)* |
| 321 | Radnor, County |
| 322 | Hartlepool |
| 323 | Gateshead |
| 324 | South Shields |
| 325 | *Dunbarton, County* |
| 326 | Batley |
| 327 | Luton |
| 328 | Newcastle-under-Lyme |
| 329 | Stirling, County |
| 330 | Peterborough, County of the |
| | Liberty of |
| 331 | Crewe |
| 332-340 | *Yorks, East Riding* |
| 341-343 | Kent, County |
| 344-345 | *Ditto (obsolete)* |
| 346 | London, County |
| 347 | *Kent, County* |
| 348 | Kent, County |
| 349 | London, County |
| 350 | *Kent, County* |
| 351 | Unappropriated |
| 352-353 | *Kent, County* |
| 354 | Kent, County |
| 355-356 | *Kent, County* |
| 357 | Kent, County |
| * 358 | Tunbridge Wells |
| 359 | *Kent, County* |
| 360 | London, County |
| 361 | Clackmannan, County |
| 362 | Stirling |
| 363 | Selkirk, County |
| 364 | *Pittenweem* |
| 365 | *Lostwithiel* |
| 366 | Hereford |
| 367 | Oxford, County |
| * 368 | Truro |
| * 369 | St Albans |
| * 370 | Smethwick |
| * 374 | Unappropriated |
| * 375 | Folkestone |
| 376 | *Great Torrington* |
| 377 | Barnstaple |
| 378 | Bridgwater |
| 379 | Burton-on-Trent |
| 380 | Elgin |
| 381 | Glossop |
| 382 | Gloucester |
| 383 | Merioneth, County |
| 384 | Stockport |
| 385 | Surrey, County |
| 386 | London, County |
| 387-388 | Surrey, County |
| * 389 | Unappropriated |
| * 390 | Unappropriated |
| 391 | Surrey, County |
| 392 | Carlisle |
| 393 | Accrington |
| 394-395 | *Hertford, County* |
| 396 | Hertford, County |
| 397-399 | *Ditto (obsolete)* |
| 400-401 | Leicester, County |
| 402 | *Ditto (obsolete)* |
| 403-407 | Leicester, County |
| 408-410 | Gloucester, County |
| * 411 | *Ditto (obsolete)* |
| * 412-415 | Unappropriated |
| 416 | Lancaster |
| 417 | Ashton-under-Lyne |
| 418 | Chesterfield |
| 419 | *Hertford* |
| 420 | Pembroke, County |
| * 421 | Unappropriated |
| 422 | Forfar |
| 423 | Kincardine, County |
| 424 | Oldham |
| 425 | *Marlborough* |
| 426 | Berwick, County |
| 427 | Cambridge |
| 428 | Montgomery, County |
| 429 | *Pontefract* |
| 430 | *Rye* |
| 431 | *Lydd* |
| 432 | *Romney Marsh, Liberty* |
| 433 | *Forres* |
| 434 | *Brecon* |
| 435 | Warwick |
| 436 | *Haverfordwest* |
| 437 | Stockton-on-Tees |
| 438 | *Dunfermline* |
| 439 | Doncaster |
| 440 | Tiverton |
| 441 | *Flint, County* |
| 442-444 | Flint, County |
| 445 | Hawick |
| 446 | *Lichfield* |
| 447 | Portsmouth |
| 448 | Leith |
| 449-452 | *Berks, County* |
| 453 | Berks, County |
| 454 | *Ditto (obsolete)* |
| 455 | Berks, County |
| 456 | Zetland, Lordship |
| 457 | *Carmarthen, County* |
| 458-459 | Carmarthen, County |
| 460 | *Ditto (obsolete)* |
| 461 | *Essex, County* |
| 462 | New Romney |
| 463 | *Ripon, City* |
| 464 | Wilts, County |
| 465 | Caithness, County |
| 466 | *Maidenhead* |
| 467 | Rotherham |
| 468 | Ayr |
| 469 | *Suffolk, East* |
| 470 | Morley |
| 471 | Hamilton |
| 472 | Bacup |
| 473 | Dunbar |
| 474-476 | Warwick, County |
| 477 | Burnley |
| 478 | St Helens |
| 479 | Midlothian, County |
| 480 | West Ham |
| 481 | Neath |
| 482 | *Surrey, County* |
| 483 | Croydon |
| 484 | *Hertford, County* |
| 485 | Hanley |
| 486 | Peterborough |
| 487 | Dundee |
| 488 | Arbroath |
| 489 | Unappropriated |
| 490 | Bristol |
| 491 | Macclesfield |
| 492 | Congleton |
| 493-494 | Nottingham, County |
| 495 | Preston, Borough |
| 496 | Middlesborough |
| 497-499 | Denbigh, County |
| 500 | Rochdale |
| 501-506 | Northumberland |
| 507 | Rochester |
| 508 | *Essex, County* |
| 509-510 | Essex, County |
| 511 | Winchester |
| 512-513 | Monmouth, County |
| 514 | Kendal |
| 515-517 | Carnarvon, County |
| 518-519 | *Ditto (obsolete)* |
| 520 | Isle of Wight, County |
| 521 | Dudley |
| 522-524 | London, County |
| 521 | Dumbarton |
| 525-526 | Northampton, County |
| 527 | Yorks, East Riding |
| 528-529 | Lincoln, County |
| 530 | Leamington |
| 531 | Rutland, County |
| 532 | Grimsby |
| 533 | Rathmines (Co. Dublin) |
| 534 | Worcester, County |
| 535-536 | Aberdeen, County |
| 537 | *Ditto (obsolete)* |
| 538 | Peebles, County |
| 539-544 | Unappropriated |
| 545 | York |
| 546 | Kirkcaldy |
| 547 | Banbury |
| 548 | Ryde, Isle of Wight |
| 549 | Guildford |
| 550-552 | Norfolk, County |
| 553 | Blackpool |
| 554 | Haddington, County |
| 555 | Airdrie |
| 556 | Shrewsbury |
| 557 | Haddington |
| 558 | Lincoln, County |
| | (Parts of Holland) |
| 559-561 | Southampton, County |
| 562 | Bury |
| 563 | Monmouth, County |
| 564 | Inverness |
| 565 | Cambridge, County |
| 566 | Argyll, County |
| 567S | Salop, County |
| 567N | Salop, County |
| 568 | Ross and Cromarty, |
| | County |
| 569 | Dover |
| 570-571 | Cardigan, County |
| 572 | Reigate |
| 573 | *Folkestone* |
| 574 | Wilts, County |
| 575-576 | Somerset, County |
| 577 | *Ditto (obsolete)* |
| 578 | Unappropriated |
| 579 | *Portsmouth* |
| 580 | Gravesend |
| 581 | Campbeltown |
| 582 | Bournemouth |
| 583 | *Devon, County (obsolete)* |
| 584-588 | Devon, County |
| 589 | Middlesex, County |
| 590 | Wakefield |
| 591 | Halifax |
| 592 | Dewsbury |
| 593 | Wigtown, County |
| 594 | Falkirk |
| 595 | Wigtown |
| 596 | *Fraserburgh* |
| 597 | West Hartlepool |
| 598 | Hyde |
| 599-600 | Essex, County |
| 601-610 | Unappropriated |
| 611 | Kingstown (Co. |
| | Dublin) |
| 612 | Ballsbridge (Co. |
| | Dublin) |
| 613 | Unappropriated |
| 614 | North Berwick |
| 615 | Dublin, City |
| 620 | Carmarthen |
| 621 | Peebles, County and |
| | Burgh |
| 622 | Durham |
| 624 | Yorks, East Riding |
| 625 | Northampton |
| 626 | Dundee |
| Exon. | Exeter |

31

# FURTHER READING

Berriman, A. E. *Historical Metrology*. Dent, 1953.
Biggs, N. *English Weights*. White House Publications, 1992.
Chaney, H. J. *Our Weights and Measures*. Eyre & Spottiswoode, 1897.
Chisholm, H. W. *Weighing and Measuring*. Macmillan, 1877.
Connor, R. D. *The Weights and Measures of England*. HMSO, 1987.
Connor, R. D., and Simpson, A. D. C. *The Weights and Measures of Scotland*. HMSO, 1993, for National Museums of Scotland.
Dent, H. C. *Old English Wool Weights*. H. W. Hunt, Norwich, 1927.
Ganeri, A. *The Story of Weights and Measures*. Oxford University Press, 1997.
Kisch, B. *Scales and Weights*. Yale University Press, 1965.
Klein, H. A. *The Science of Measurement: A Historical Survey*. Dover Publications, 1989.
*Libra*. The Institute of Trading Standards Administration. Volumes 1 to 10, 1962–74.
Nicholson, E. *Men and Measures*. Smith, Elder & Company, 1912.
Stevenson, M. *Weights and Measures of the City of Winchester*. Winchester Museums Service, 1991.
Stevenson, M. *Weight Stamping by the Worshipful Company of Founders and the City of London*. Founders' Hall, EC1A 7HT, 1991.
Zupke, B. E. *A Dictionary of English Weights and Measures*. University of Wisconsin Press, 1968.

# PLACES TO VISIT

Many county museums have displays of weights and measures, some with examples of standards issued by Henry VII and Elizabeth I. Displays may be altered and readers are advised to telephone before visiting to check that relevant items are on show, as well as to find out opening times

*Anne of Cleves House Museum*, 52 Southover High Street, Lewes, East Sussex BN7 1JA. Telephone: 01273 474610. Website: www.sussexpast.co.uk

*Ashmolean Museum*, Beaumont Street, Oxford OX1 2PH. Telephone: 01865 278000. Website: www.ashmol.ox.ac.uk

*Avery Historical Museum*, Foundry Lane, Smethwick, Warley, West Midlands B66 2LP. Telephone: 08709 034343. Website: www.averyberkel.com

*Bank of England Museum*, Threadneedle Street, London EC2R 8AH. Telephone: 020 7601 5491. Website: www.bankofengland.co.uk/museum

*Birmingham Museum and Art Gallery*, Chamberlain Square, Birmingham B3 3DH. Telephone: 0121 303 2834. Website: www.birmingham.gov.uk/bmag

*Bridewell Museum*, Bridewell Alley, Norwich NR2 1AQ. Telephone: 01603 667228. Website: www.norfolk.gov.uk/tourism/museums

*Cambridge and County Folk Museum*, 2/3 Castle Street, Cambridge CB3 0AQ. Telephone: 01223 355159. Website: www.folkmuseum.org.uk

*Ceredigion Museum*, Coliseum, Terrace Road, Aberystwyth SY23 2AQ. Telephone: 01970 633088. Website: www.ceredigion.gov.uk

*Derby Museum and Art Gallery*, The Strand, Derby DE1 1BS. Telephone 01332 716659. Website: www.derby.gov.uk/museums

*Fife Folk Museum*, Weigh House, High Street, Ceres, Cupar, Fife KY15 5NF. Telephone: 01334 828180.

*Kingston Museum and Art Gallery*, Wheatfield Way, Kingston upon Thames, Surrey KT1 2PS. Telephone: 020 8546 5386. Website: www.kingston.gov.uk/museum

*Laing Art Gallery*, New Bridge Street, Newcastle upon Tyne NE1 8AG. Telephone: 0191 232 7734. Website: www.twmuseums.org.uk

*Lawrence House Museum*, 9 Castle Street, Launceston, Cornwall PL15 8BA. Telephone: 01566 773277.

*Museum of London*, 150 London Wall, London EC2Y 5HN. Telephone: 020 7600 3699. Website: www.museumoflondon.org.uk

*Perth Museum and Art Gallery*, 78 George Street, Perth PH1 5LB. Telephone: 01738 632488. Website: www.pkc.co.uk

*Royal Museum of Scotland*, Chambers Street, Edinburgh EH1 1JF. Telephone: 0131 225 7534. Website: www.nms.ac.uk

*Salisbury and South Wiltshire Museum*, The King's House, 65 The Close, Salisbury, Wiltshire SP1 2EN. Telephone: 01722 332151. Website: www.salisburymuseum.org.uk

*Science Museum*, Exhibition Road, South Kensington, London SW7 2DD. Telephone: 0870 870 4771. Website: www.sciencemuseum.org

*Shrewsbury Museum and Art Gallery*, Rowley's House, Barker Street, Shrewsbury, Shropshire SY1 1QH. Telephone: 01743 361196. Website: www.shrewsburymuseums.com

*Stamford Museum*, Broad Street, Stamford, Lincolnshire PE9 1PJ. Telephone: 01780 766317. Website: www.lincolnshire.gov.uk

*Tolson Memorial Museum*, Ravensknowle Park, Huddersfield, West Yorkshire HD5 8DJ. Telephone: 01484 223830. Website: www.kirkleesmc.gov.uk

*Towner Art Gallery and Local Museum*, High Street, Old Town, Eastbourne, East Sussex BN22 8BB. Telephone: 01323 411688. Website: www.eastbourne.org

*Westgate Museum*, High Street,Winchester, Hampshire. Telephone: 01962 848269. Website: www.winchester.gov.uk/heritage

*Wiltshire Heritage Museum*, 41 Long Street, Devizes, Wiltshire SN10 1NS. Telephone: 01380 727369. Website: www.wiltshireheritage.org.uk

*Wisbech and Fenland Museum*, Museum Square, Wisbech, Cambridgeshire PE13 1ES. Telephone: 01945 583817.

*Yorkshire Museum*, Museum Gardens, York YO1 7FR. Telephone: 01904 551800. Website: www.york.gov.uk